Dirt & Grime

LIKE YOU'VE NEVER SEEN!

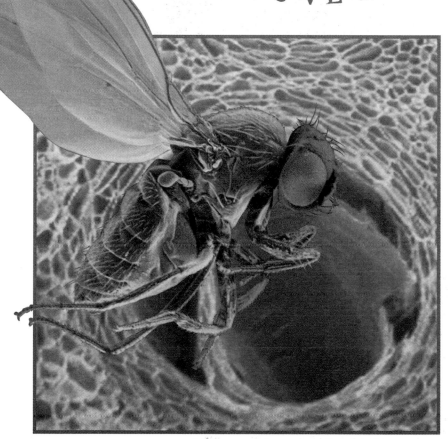

Vicki Cobb

Scholastic Inc.

New York   Toronto   London   Auckland   Sydney

For Rachel Petersen Cobb

Photo Credits

Magnifications of the images are in parenthesis following the page number.

Cover: Dennis Kunkel, Kailua, Hawaii/Phototake: front (x436,800), back top left (x5880), back top right (x172,200), center (x299,250), bottom right (x16,065); Andrew Syred/SPL/Photo Researchers: back bottom left (x29,925).

Interior: G.J. Hills, John Innes Institutes/SPL/Photo Researchers: 5 bottom (x10,920,000,000); Dennis Kunkel, Kailua, Hawaii/Phototake: 1 silhouette (x3528), 3 (x32,602), 4 (x483,000), 6 (x609,000), 7 top (x11,602), 7 bottom (x10,237), 8 left (x11,025), 8 right (x20,790), 9 (x352,537), 10 (x5,082,000), 11 (x1,312,500), 12 (x51,187), 13 (x598,500), 14 (x27,562,500), 15 (x120,750), 17 (x7,696,080), 18 (x383,250), 19 top (x105,472), 19 bottom (x302,400), 20 (x94,710), 21 (x36,120), 22 (x4200), 23 (x8032), 27 (x27,300), 28 (x310,537), 29 (x354,375), 32 black and white (x14,437), 32 color (x6562); Charles Miller: 16 (strobe photo); Secchi-Lecaque/Roussel-UCLAF/CNRI/SPL/Photo Researchers: 16 (x6,363,000); Andrew Syred/SPL/Photo Researchers: 24 (x384,300), 25 (x93,240), 1 (x26,460) and 26 (x29,400), 30 (x26,775), 31 (x1,092,000); J & L Weber/Peter Arnold: 5 top (x33,600).

BOOK DESIGN BY KEVIN CALLAHAN/BNGO BOOKS

Library of Congress Cataloging-in-Publication Data

Cobb, Vicki
Dirt and grime, like you've never seen / by Vicki Cobb.
p. cm.
Includes index.
ISBN 0-590-92666-7
Summary: Using scanning electron microscopy, studies household dirt, dust, and germs, and the substances that are used to get rid of them.
1. Scanning electron microscopy - Juvenile literature.
[1. Scanning electron microscopy. 2. Microscopy.] I. Title.
QH212.S3C63 1998   97-9336
502'.8'25 - dc21   CIP
                                                                          AC

12 11 10 9 8 7 6 5 4 3 2 1   8 9/9 0 1 2 3/0

Printed in the U.S.A.
First printing, January 1998

CONTENTS

DIRT

Want to touch something dirty? "No, thank you," you say. But sometimes you can't avoid it. If you've ever gardened, scrubbed floors, or built sand castles, you've gotten your hands into dirt. You can also get your hands in dirt if you prepare samples of it to look at under a microscope. Up close, dirt is different from anything you ever imagined. It tells stories about the earth and reveals secrets of its treasures. It's fascinating, to say the least.

In this book we'll take a closer look at dirt and grime and other things many people find very unpleasant, even unhealthy. Most of the pictures have been taken with a ***scanning electron microscope,*** which can magnify a surface up to three hundred thousand times larger than its actual size. Since common dirt is a part of the earth, we'll start by zooming in on the stuff the earth is made of.

JOURNEY FROM THE DEPTHS OF THE EARTH

Miles beneath the earth's crust a mixture of rock and trapped gases, called *magma*, is so hot that it's a liquid. When there is a crack in the crust, the magma begins traveling to the surface, where it erupts, forming a volcano. On May 18, 1980, at 8:32 in the morning, Mount St. Helens, in the state of Washington, erupted with a force equal to ten million tons of dynamite. Ash and rock were thrown miles into the air. One of the rocks from that eruption is the subject of this *scanning electron micrograph*, or *SEM*, for short.

If it looks like it's full of holes, that's because it is. This rock is called *pumice* (from a word meaning "foam" in Latin) and it is found at many volcanoes. The magma had many gases dissolved in it, much the way carbon dioxide is dissolved in a can of soda. As the gas-containing magma moved up on its trip to the surface, the gas came out of the rock and formed tiny bubbles, just as gas bubbles form in soda when you pop the top. During the eruption the air quickly cooled the magma, the bubbles were frozen into place, and, *ta-da*, pumice!

Pumice is a lightweight rock, light enough to float. Its rough surface can be used to smooth and polish and it's often used to sand dead skin off your feet. You can buy a piece of pumice and see how it floats while you're washing in the bathtub.

NOT-SO-CHEAP DIRT

A diamond is the hardest substance on Earth. No material on Earth can scratch a diamond except another diamond. Why? A clue to its hardness is in the structure of the diamond crystal that shows in this picture. A diamond is a crystal of the element *carbon.* Each carbon atom is strongly bonded to four other carbon atoms in the shape of a four-sided pyramid with a square base. The pyramids fit together like blocks, pointing up and down. The combination of the strong bond between carbon atoms and the blocklike structure of the pyramids causes the diamond's extreme hardness. In this photo, taken with polarized light through an ordinary light microscope, you can see the triangular sides of the pyramids. The repeated triangles show the internal structure of the diamond crystal.

Like pumice, diamonds are formed way beneath the earth's crust under extreme heat and pressure. All diamonds are, at the least, almost a billion years old and many are more than three billion years old. They were transported toward the surface in diamond "pipes," tubelike columns containing a rather ordinary magma. Only twenty percent of the diamonds mined today can be used for jewelry. Most diamonds are used as cutting and polishing tools in industry.

This very thin slice of a gold crystal, also mined from the earth, shows the remarkable magnifying power of the electron microscope. This is an enlargement of a photo that magnifies the crystal *sixteen million* times. This degree of magnification is only possible with a souped-up version of the electron microscope. Since electron micrographs are only in black and white, this picture was later colored and made clearer by a computer. Each yellow blob represents one gold atom. The regular arrangement of the atoms shows up when you look at an actual gold crystal, which is shaped like a cube.

WORTH ITS SALT

The earth is full of minerals—compounds that are crystals when they are in their purest form. This is a blue-colored SEM of salt—one of the most important of the earth's minerals. Notice that salt crystals are cubes. Use a magnifying lens to look at some table salt and you'll see the same thing.

At one time in human history, salt was more valuable than oil is today. It is absolutely necessary to our diet and early communities were established in desert areas near salt deposits. The words "salary" and "sale" come from a time when salt was used as money. Salt is cheap today because we have found many ways of producing it from mines and from seawater.

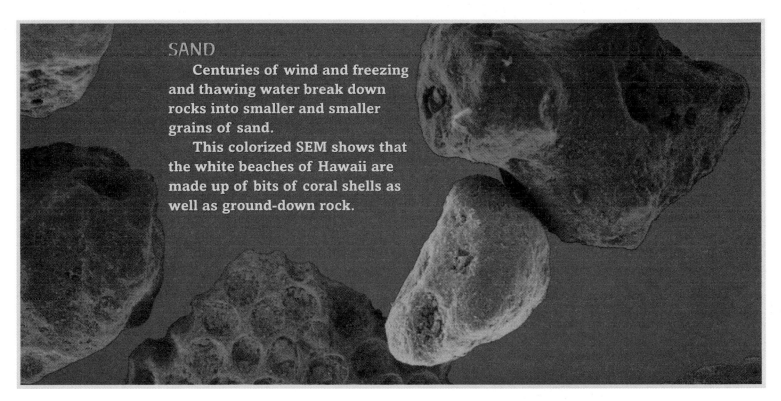

SAND

Centuries of wind and freezing and thawing water break down rocks into smaller and smaller grains of sand.

This colorized SEM shows that the white beaches of Hawaii are made up of bits of coral shells as well as ground-down rock.

SOIL

Add decayed vegetable matter, called **humus,** to sand and you have a fertile soil capable of providing a nourishing environment for new plant growth. **Microbes**, microscopic living things like bacteria, yeast, and mold, are responsible for breaking down formerly living material, like the wood fibers and leaves in this SEM.

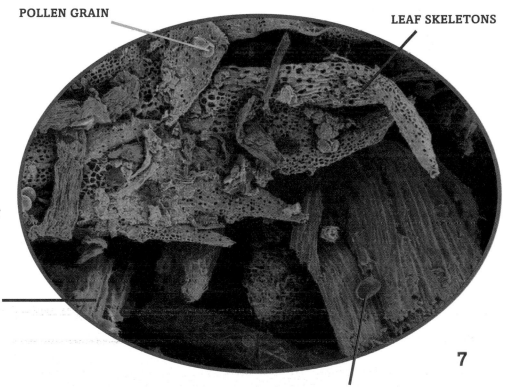

POLLEN GRAIN

LEAF SKELETONS

WOOD FIBERS

MINERAL PARTICLES

7

GRIME

Grime is dirt stuck to surfaces—all kinds of surfaces, from clothing to countertops to floors to teeth. Cleaning grime off surfaces is a never-ending task. Where does all the grime come from? How can we get rid of it? These are questions that scientists investigate. The answers are used by the multibillion-dollar industry that makes products for keeping clean and cleaning up.

The scanning electron microscope is particularly useful for shedding light on grime. Get ready for some good reasons to scrub.

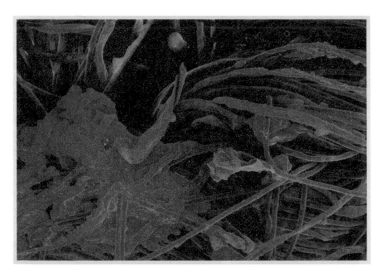

YOU'RE NOT SO CLEAN, EITHER

Your ear funnels sound down a canal to your eardrum. The outer part of this canal is coated with wax to protect the canal and your eardrum from water, dust, and foreign particles. As earwax accumulates, it moves from the ear canal to the outer ear, where it can be removed by gently wiping it with a cotton swab. In this SEM, the earwax is the yellowish clumps sticking to the grayish cotton fibers. It is a mistake to push anything into your ear canal because it can force the wax farther in, where it can form a plug and interfere with hearing.

RING AROUND THE COLLAR

The rough fibers of a T-shirt rub against your skin. It's no surprise that skin cells rub off and cling to the fibers. Your skin is supposed to shed. In fact, you shed almost a million dead skin cells every hour of your life. This SEM gives you an up-close and personal look at ring-around-the-collar on the neck of a blue-colored T-shirt.

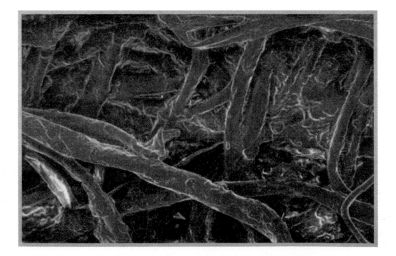

Tooth enamel is the hardest surface in the body. It should withstand a lifetime of chewing. Except there's a danger from a whitish scum, called **plaque,** that makes your teeth feel furry in the morning. This is an SEM portrait of plaque. Plaque is made up of **bacteria**—one-celled microbes—and proteins from saliva. Your mouth contains six hundred different species of bacteria and most of them are friendly. Since bacteria are living things, they take in food and give off wastes.

Plaque bacteria happen to like sugar. They get it from food you eat. Their waste is an acid, which is good news and bad. The good news is that the acid can prevent bad bacteria from getting a toehold in your mouth. The bad news is that it can eat into the tough enamel and cause cavities.

If you brush off the plaque, floss between your teeth, and visit your dentist regularly, you can keep things under control.

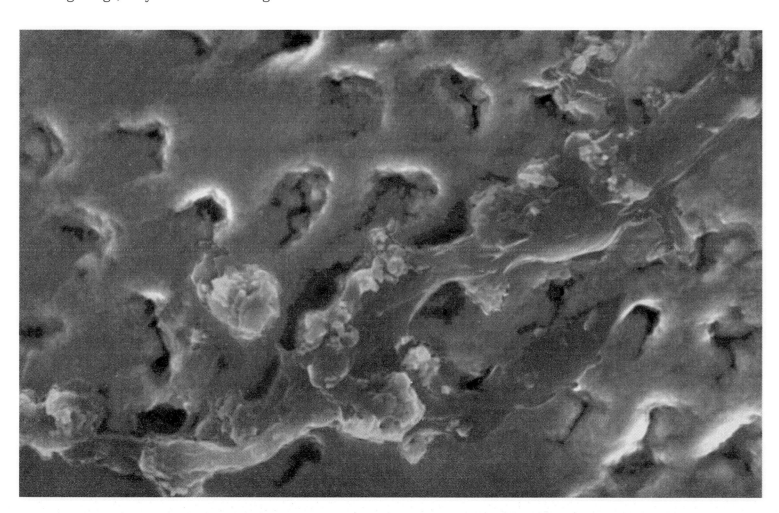

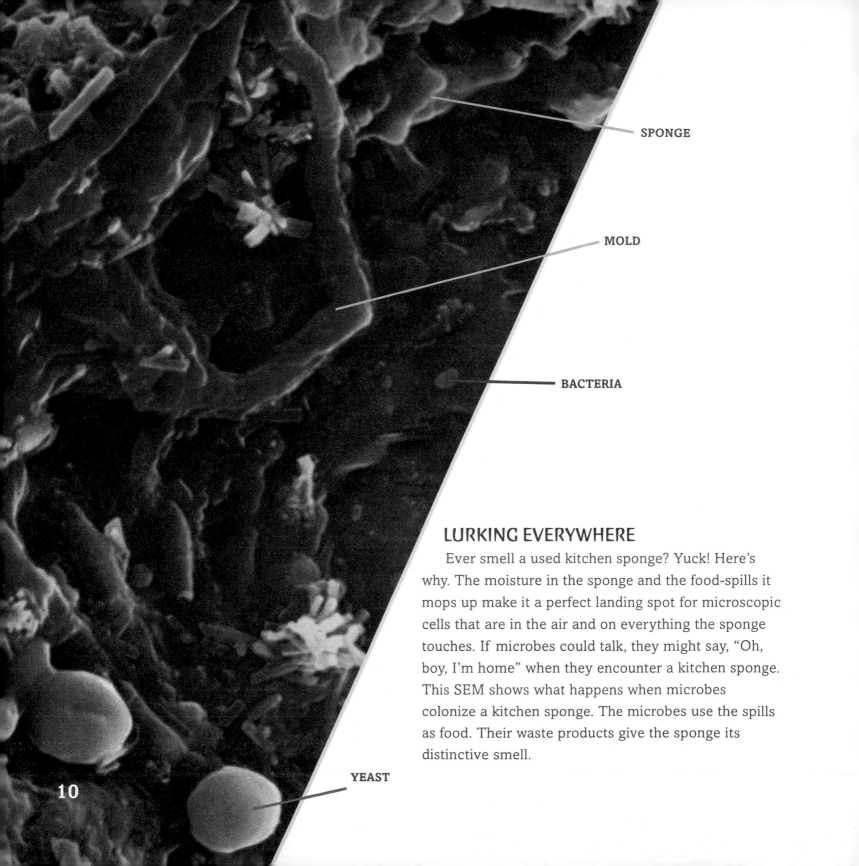

SPONGE

MOLD

BACTERIA

YEAST

LURKING EVERYWHERE

Ever smell a used kitchen sponge? Yuck! Here's why. The moisture in the sponge and the food-spills it mops up make it a perfect landing spot for microscopic cells that are in the air and on everything the sponge touches. If microbes could talk, they might say, "Oh, boy, I'm home" when they encounter a kitchen sponge. This SEM shows what happens when microbes colonize a kitchen sponge. The microbes use the spills as food. Their waste products give the sponge its distinctive smell.

Even the pits and grooves on a plastic cutting board catch enough moisture to grow this garden of microbes.

Scientists have recently discovered that we have completely underestimated the importance of bacteria. Anywhere there is water with a temperature between about 20 and 250 degrees Fahrenheit there are bacteria. This means at the North and South Poles, the deepest part of the sea, in hot springs, in cracks in volcanoes, and even miles beneath the earth's surface. In spite of their small size—millions of them fit easily in a drop of water—there are so many on Earth that their weight adds up. If you could weigh all the living material on Earth—plants, animals, insects, and bacteria—bacteria would be more than eight pounds out of every ten. Some scientists have stated that microbes could weigh more than the total weight of the earth itself!

Anywhere you see grime in cracks, you can safely guess it's microbes.

MOLD FIBERS

BACTERIA

MOLD SPORES

CUTTING BOARD

11

DUST

What are the sizes of dust particles? What are they made of? How long do they take to settle? These are some questions asked by scientists. The scanning electron microscope helps find answers.

A house needs to be cleaned even if no one lives in it. Air is full of particles, and sooner or later they settle on surfaces as dust. You can see some dust particles floating in the air in a stream of sunlight. The smallest particles the human eye can see are about forty microns in size. A human hair is one hundred microns thick. Over ninety-nine percent of the particles found in the air are less than one micron in size. Tobacco smoke is made up of invisible particles about one-tenth of a micron in size. But when you have enough of them, you can see them. In spite of their tiny size, tobacco smoke particles will eventually settle as dust, although it can take up to two days for them to fall to the floor from a height of six feet.

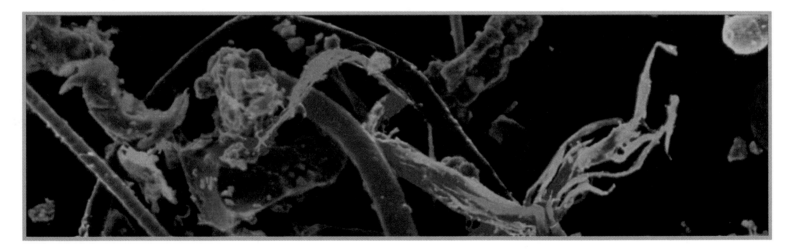

AN ORDINARY PICTURE

No, this is not modern art. This is a colorized SEM of common household dust. You can see colored fibers that are shed from clothing, furniture, and bedding. A grain of pollen is colored yellow. It drifted in through an open door or window. Hairs are colored rust and dark brown. The small brownish bits are most likely dead human skin cells and mineral material. Your skin and the skins of the members of your family are major contributors to the dust in your house.

SOMETHING TO SNEEZE AT

These are not space objects; they're air objects. They are ragweed pollen grains, and if you inhale them, they'll start you sneezing. *Pollen* is the male part of flowers. When it unites with the female part of the plant, seeds will form. These ragweed pollen grains have tiny points so that they can dig into a target flower—or into the delicate tissue inside your nose and sinuses.

Ragweed causes hay fever— the most common of all allergy diseases, with seventy-two million sufferers in the United States. Wind and air currents can carry the pollen more than ten miles from the plant—a hardy weed that grows in ditches and fields and unweeded gardens. A lot of people will be miserable throughout the summer. Relief finally comes when the first major frost kills the plants.

13

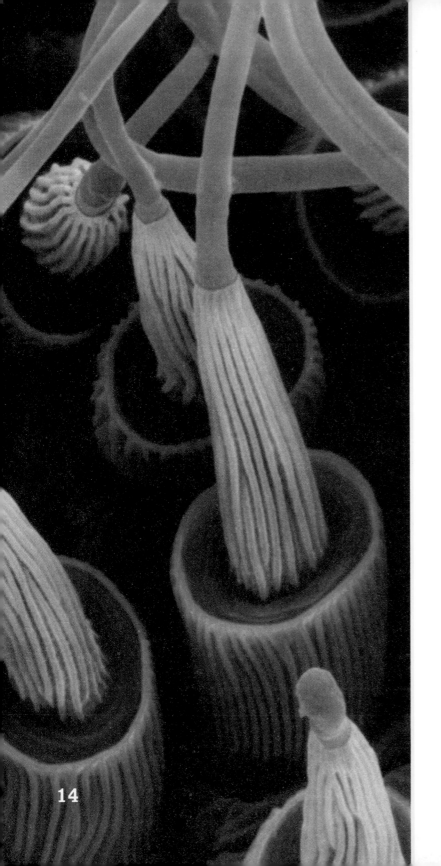

COBWEBS

Part of the job of dusting is getting to those cobwebs in corners and hard-to-reach places. This SEM shows spider silk coming out of a spider's *spinnerets,* the tube-like organs that produce spider silk. Spider silk is a protein that starts out as a liquid when it is inside a spinneret but solidifies in less than a second after it hits the air. The silk is a smooth round fiber, molded by the spinneret much as toothpaste is shaped when it's squeezed from a tube.

Spider silk is an amazing material. No metal or man-made material is as strong or as elastic. A spider silk fiber is five times stronger than a steel fiber the same size and it has twice the stretchiness of nylon. Some of a web's fibers are coated with a sticky material to make it more difficult for a trapped insect to escape. This sticky material, which is an acid, also makes a web resistant to attack by bacteria and fungi. Abandoned spiderwebs don't rot away, much to the dismay of a person with a dust rag.

CLEAN IT UP!

This is an SEM of a speck of dust on a computer *microchip*—a tiny electrical circuit that helps run high-tech electronic devices. You can see the aluminum strips on the surface that control the flow of electricity. A tiny speck of dust on a microchip is an absolute no-no—a monkey wrench fouling up the works. So microchip manufacturers go to great expense to put their chips together in rooms—called *clean rooms*—that are virtually dust-free.

This is no easy task. The average room has a million or more invisible particles in every cubic foot of air. A "dirty" clean room has only a hundred thousand dust particles per cubic foot and the cleanest clean room has only one particle of dust per cubic foot. How do they get the dust out? By passing air into the room through pleated filters with holes that are smaller than the smallest dust particles. The pleats give the filter depth to trap more particles. The air in a clean room is under a higher pressure than normal, so when a door opens, the air blows out, not in. The cleanest clean rooms are inside a less-clean clean room. If you wanted to enter, you would have to put on a bunny suit that covers you completely, with gloves, booties, hairnet, eyeglasses, and face mask. Then you would have to take an air shower to blow off any clinging particles. Even with all this, some dirt manages to get in. During the manufacturing process, chips are cleaned many times.

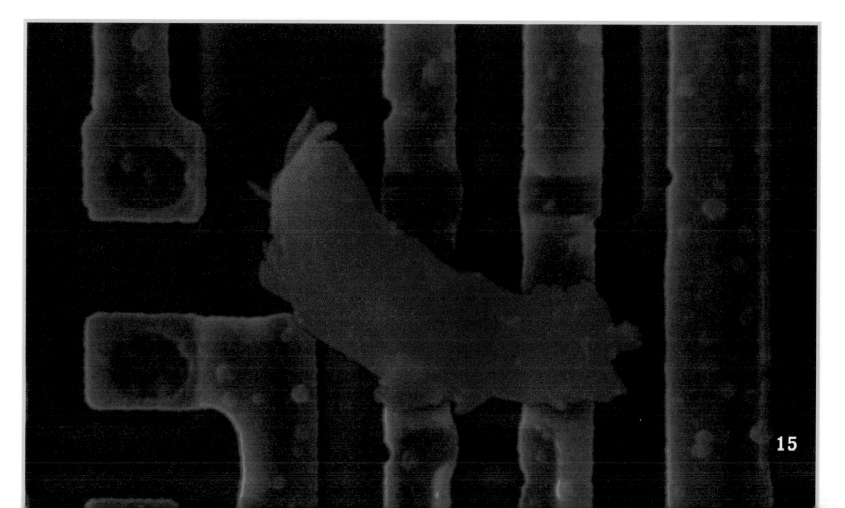

GERMS

ACH⊚⊚!, a sneeze explodes out of your nose and mouth. A scientist captured the moment using a rapidly flashing light called a *strobe*. A sneeze is a reflex that lets you get rid of undesirable material. It contains about five thousand droplets of water mucus from the lining of your nose and windpipe. Each droplet contains microbes—viruses and bacteria. If you have a cold or other sickness, viruses expelled when you sneeze can infect others if they breathe in your droplets. A sneeze exiting a nose has been clocked at slightly more than one hundred miles an hour and it is powerful enough to send the droplets a distance of twelve feet. They land on surfaces people touch. So to prevent droplet infection, cover your mouth and nose when you sneeze and, since you don't know what you've touched, wash your hands before eating.

VIRUSES

The scanning electron microscope shows what's in the droplets. These are flu viruses, of a variety that has many different shapes. A virus has an outside shell of protein, colored purple in this picture, surrounding red-colored genetic material—something like a free-floating cell nucleus. It is an incomplete cell, unable to move or take in food. It travels in suspended animation, from one person to another, through droplets coughed or sneezed in the air. Once inside a new individual, flu viruses invade the cells of the respiratory system and use the host cells' "machinery" to reproduce themselves. When a host cell is full of viruses, it ruptures and dies, spilling out viruses that attack other cells.

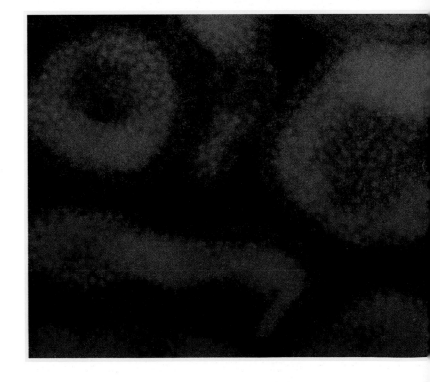

BACTERIA

Bacteria are another kind of germ. This SEM shows two of the three basic shapes of bacteria. The violet-colored rod-shaped cells, called *E. coli,* come from the human colon, where they make up about half the weight of the bowel. Scientists check water for sewage pollution by testing for *E. coli.*

The round, orange-colored cells are *streptococci.* Some kinds of streptococci can cause disease, such as strep throat, but most live inside us without harming us. The third shape is a spiral, called *spirochete,* not shown in this picture. Spirochetes cause diseases like Lyme disease.

Some of the bacteria in this SEM are dividing in half, one way they reproduce themselves. The rod-shaped bacteria grow many times longer than their original length and then split in half. The streptococci split down the middle before separating. Under ideal conditions, bacteria double their number every twenty minutes. That means if you start with one cell, there are eight cells after one hour, 8,192 after three hours, and 33,554,432 after eight hours!

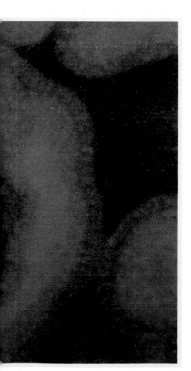

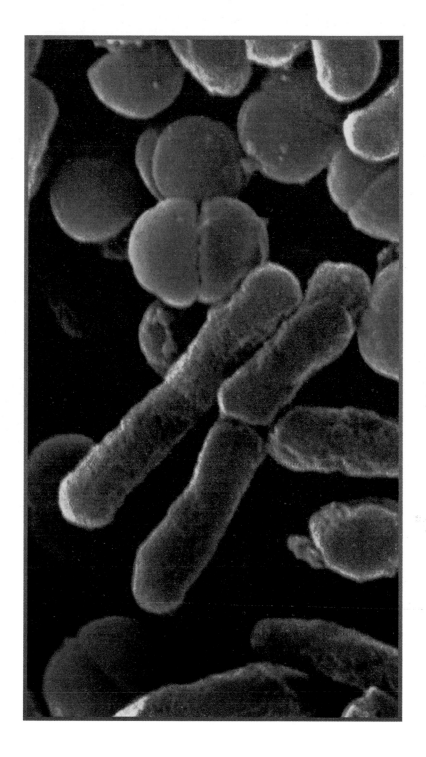

MOLD

Floating in the air, along with bacteria and viruses, are tiny seedlike **spores.** If the spores happen to land on the right surface—one that contains some moisture—they will sprout and become spore-producing mold colonies. Molds are multicellular organisms that cannot make their own food like green plants, and they cannot take food into themselves like animals. Instead, they secrete enzymes outside their cell walls that digest the substance on which they live so that they can absorb nourishment into their cells. Some mold colonies are **parasites**—they live off other living organisms. And some exist on dead organisms.

ROTTEN STUFF

This is one sick lettuce leaf. As it was growing, it was infected with a white powdery mildew. The threadlike branching structures are called **hyphae.** Food-absorbing hyphae penetrate the living leaf, ultimately destroying it. Another kind of hyphae, called **fertile hyphae,** extends up into the air. Fertile hyphae have sections full of tiny spores enclosed within a cell wall. When the spores are released to the air, new growth spreads to other leaves. Powdery mildew is not a happy sight for farmers.

In this SEM you can see that the lettuce leaf is dotted with an occasional **stomate**—an opening in the leaf that looks like a pair of lips. Among other jobs, stomates control the amount of water vapor that escapes from the leaves. As water evaporates from the leaves, replacement water is drawn up from the roots.

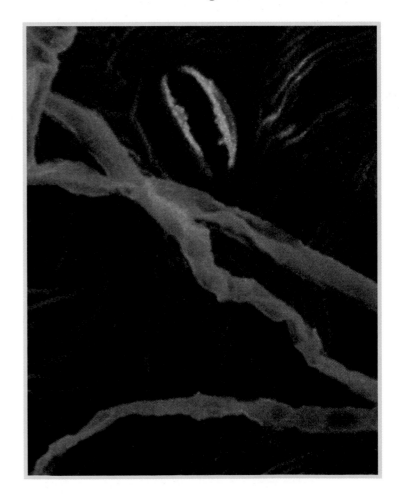

BREAD MOLD

This SEM shows the fruiting body of a black mold, colored blue in this micrograph. It contains chains of tiny ball-like spores. This mold grows on bread as well as other vegetable matter.

Blue mold is called **penicillium,** from the Latin word meaning "little brush." The SEM below shows it growing on an orange but it also grows on bread. The blue-colored balls are spores at the end of tube-shaped cells that support them. You probably think food infected with this mold should be thrown out. But if you like blue cheeses or Roquefort cheese, you do eat this stuff. Moldy cheese is made by mixing *penicillium* into unripened cheese.

Penicillium is famous for another reason. In 1928 Alexander Fleming, a Scottish scientist, was about to throw away a dish containing colonies of bacteria he had been studying. He noticed that some mold had landed in the dish. Around each spot of mold was a clear area where the bacteria had been killed. The mold was

penicillium, and from this discovery came the first of many bacteria-killing antibiotic drugs, called—you guessed it—penicillin.

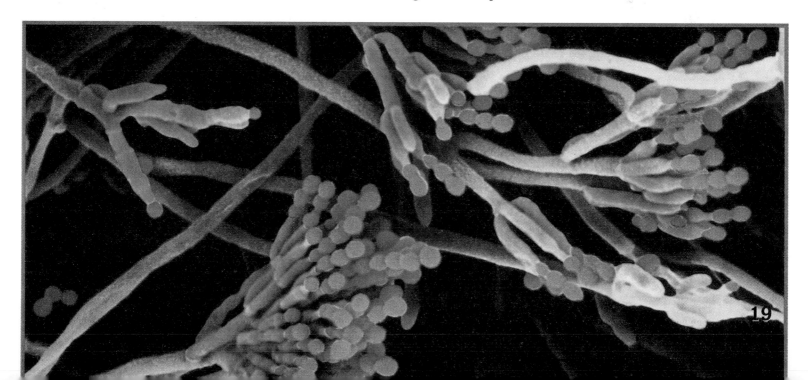

BUGS

Hasn't your mother told you that if you don't clean up, you'll get bugs? Well, it's true. The scanning electron microscope shows dirt-loving household bugs in fearsome detail.

DUST MITE

Nature is not wasteful. Remember all those skin cells you shed, making your contribution to household dust? Well, you've provided dinner for this critter—a genuine people-eater. Dust mites are microscopic, eight-legged distant cousins of spiders that live in mattresses and under beds, where they munch on human skin cells. In real life, they're brown. We decided to color this one purple. Females lay twenty-five to fifty eggs and a new generation hatches every three weeks. Some people have estimated that millions of dust mites live in one old mattress.

These bedbugs don't bite. But their waste particles can cause asthma attacks for people who are allergic to dust. The best weapon of defense is the vacuum cleaner.

CARPET BEETLE

This is the head of a young adult carpet beetle. In real life this bug is black, about a quarter inch in length, and is shaped something like a ladybug. It can fly and feeds on nectar and pollen, so it's not a problem for your household unless it gets in through a window and lays eggs in a rug. The immature form of a carpet beetle, its *larva*, is a destructive and hungry little creature. Carpet beetle larvae dine on dead animal and vegetable materials such as hair, wool, cotton, and leather. The larvae are about a half inch long, carrot-shaped, and fast-moving. They crawl from room to room, hiding behind baseboards and moldings. They don't like light and they have been known to devour carpets in the darkness under heavy furniture.

Carpets woven from man-made fibers are not in their diet.

21

FRUIT FLY

Ever notice the tiny flies hovering like miniature helicopters over a fruit bowl? They appear, as if by magic, wherever there are overripe fruits and vegetables. Their favorite foods are rotten bananas, baked goods containing yeast, soft drinks, and vinegar. They hang out around garbage cans, dirty mops, and empty ketchup bottles. They lay their eggs in moist, rotting food so that their tiny larvae are surrounded by food the instant they hatch.

Fruit flies have, however, made an enormous contribution to science. A fruit fly can complete a life cycle in about eight days. For this reason, they have been very useful for learning how traits, such as eye color, are inherited down through many generations. A geneticist can study forty generations of fruit flies in one year. On average, forty generations of people would take almost a thousand years.

COCKROACH

This bug is a sure sign that a home is not perfectly spotless. Cockroaches are living fossils—looking pretty much as they did 208 million years ago. In this SEM of a cockroach head, the eyes on each side are colored red. The extremely flexible antennae are coming out of the front of the head. They thrash about like whips, especially when a roach reaches a table edge. Their reflexes are about five times faster than yours, which is why they are so difficult to step on.

Cockroaches eat just about anything, from paper to scraps of food to the carcasses of other cockroaches. They can fit into extremely small cracks, where they spend seventy-five percent of their time resting. They avoid light. You can fool yourself into thinking that you're bug-free in the daytime. Just wait until you turn on the kitchen light in the middle of the night!

Cockroaches have filthy habits. They walk through their own waste and it's possible that they spread diseases. Cockroaches are not our friends.

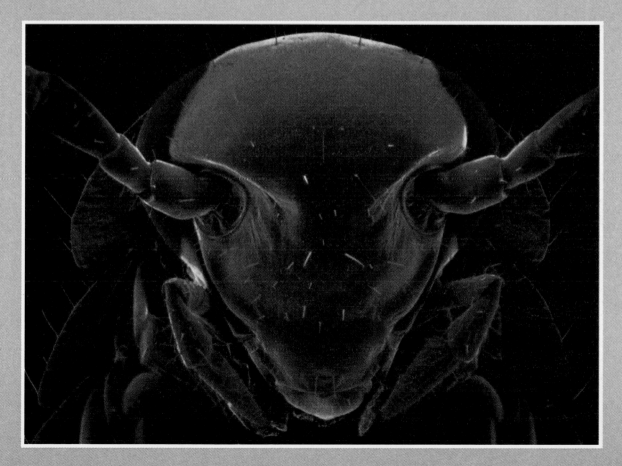

GARBAGE

The average person throws out about fifteen hundred pounds of garbage a year. What happens to it? We used to burn garbage until we found out that it polluted the air. Compost heaps are very effective for wet, biodegradable garbage. If you place garbage in a backyard pile, mold and bacteria will rot it into humus. Of course, compost heaps are not practical for city dwellers. So most garbage, at least the stuff we don't recycle, is used as landfill in huge garbage dumps. Eventually, some dumps can become parks or playgrounds.

We thought it might be interesting to fish a few things out of the garbage can and take a closer look at them through the electron microscope.

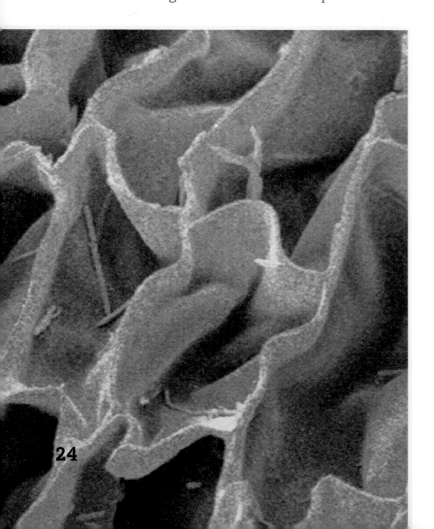

BOTTLE STOPPER

This SEM shows the cells of a cork from a bottle. Actually, what you see are the cell walls from a cork oak tree. The living material in the cells has dried up, leaving behind empty spaces. Cork cells are lined up in rows. The cell walls give it a rigid strength, not common to such lightweight material. You can tell this is a used cork because the cells are no longer rectangular. They were squeezed when the cork was put in the bottle.

Cork cells were the first cells to be seen through the microscope back in the seventeenth century. Robert Hooke, the English scientist who first saw them, named the tiny structures "cells" because they reminded him of the little rooms that monks live in, also called cells. Later, the cell came to be seen as the smallest unit of a living thing.

24

EGGSHELL

An eggshell's main job is to protect a developing chick and keep it from drying out. This SEM shows a cracked eggshell with a little bit of membrane clinging to the inside surface. An eggshell is made of the same mineral, *calcium carbonate,* that we have in our bones and teeth, and that sea creatures have in their shells. As the chick grows, it absorbs the calcium carbonate from the shell into its bones. This makes the shell thinner and allows the membrane to control the flow of gases and water vapor in and out of the shell.

Shells of eggs we eat are thick because chicks never grew in them.

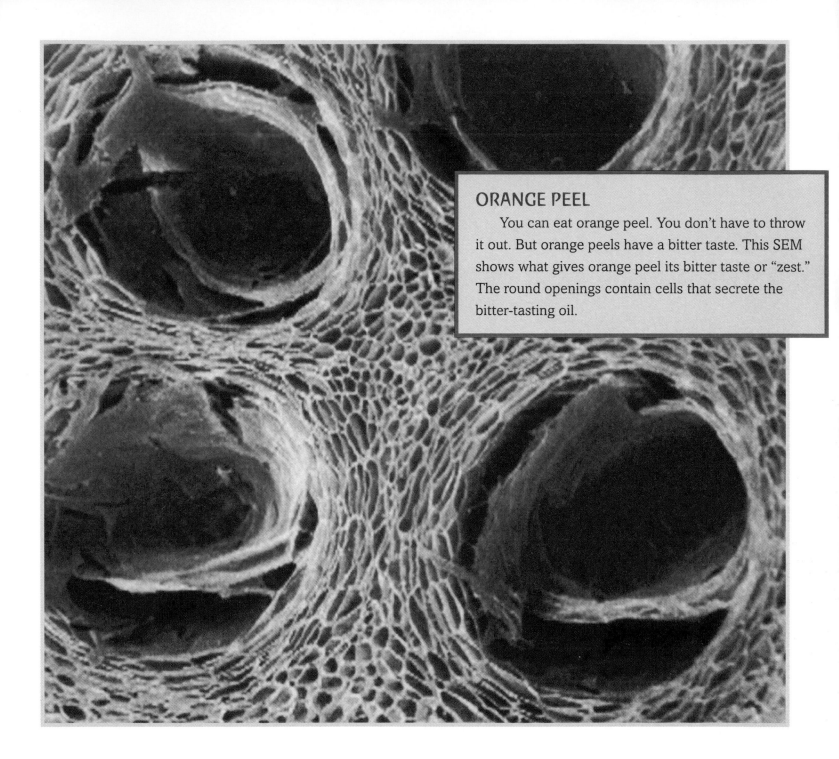

ORANGE PEEL

You can eat orange peel. You don't have to throw it out. But orange peels have a bitter taste. This SEM shows what gives orange peel its bitter taste or "zest." The round openings contain cells that secrete the bitter-tasting oil.

USED BANDAGE

There is absolutely no reason to hang on to a small adhesive bandage after your cut has healed. But let's take a close look at what you throw away. This SEM shows one of the tiny holes on the underside of the bandage that leads to some absorbent fibers. Dried blood cells from the wound have stuck to the fibers. The area surrounding the hole is the nonsticky surface that goes right over the cut.

CLEANING UP

So are you now ready to start scrubbing? Water alone won't do it. You need help. Before there was an industry producing household cleansers, people knew that rubbing, by itself, wouldn't do a very good job. You need something rough—an *abrasive*—like sandpaper, that can come to grips with surface dirt. Actually, one of the first abrasives ever used was sand. Like fighting fire with fire, dirt can be cleaned by using a kind of dirt. In addition to an abrasive, household cleansers may contain soaps to dissolve grease, bleaches to change dark colors to light, and enzymes to break up stains.

BROKEN GLASS

Broken glass can cut. So why not use tiny bits of it in cleansers? One of the best sources of natural broken glass comes from the fossils of microscopic one-celled plants called *diatoms.* The boxlike skeletons of diatoms, called *frustules,* are made of *silica*—the same stuff glass is made of. Diatoms come in a variety of beautiful geometric shapes. They settle to the bottoms of lakes and oceans, where their frustules are preserved in large deposits of white chalky material known as *diatomite.* This SEM shows the frustules and frustule fragments of several different kinds of diatoms.

Diatomite is mined for use in cleansers, filters, and abrasives. It is also used as an environmentally friendly insecticide. It is dusted on crops. When tiny, crop-destroying insects crawl over it, the frustule fragments cut them up. Their body fluids leak away and they dry out and die.

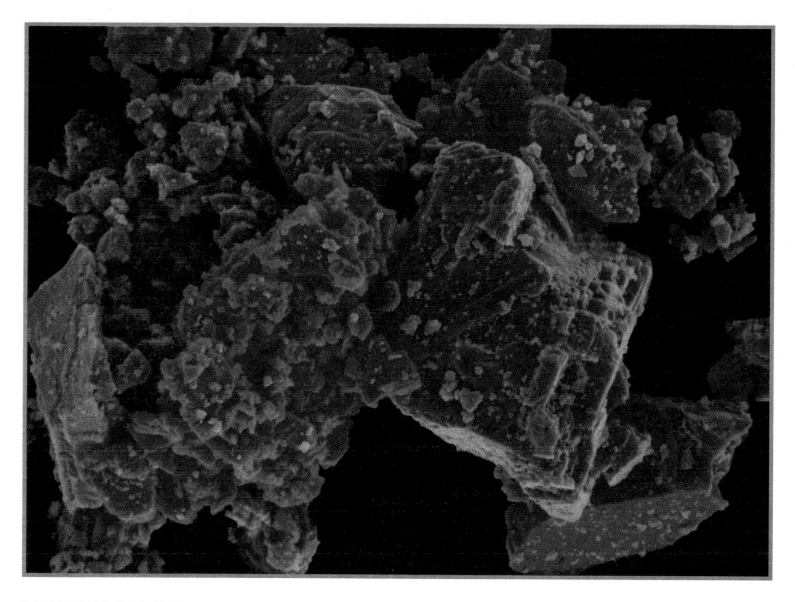

SCOURING POWDER

Calcium carbonate shows up again as a gritty mineral abrasive in this SEM of powdered household cleanser. The cleanser forms a paste with water that is used to scour the surfaces of sinks and pots and pans. In addition to the calcium carbonate, the cleanser includes a bleach, water softener, preservatives, and coloring material.

DETERGENT

This SEM shows granules of a modern laundry detergent. Some of the shells of the granules are open, revealing their stuffing of *enzymes.* Enzymes are proteins that cause chemical reactions among molecules that originally came from living things. Some enzymes in laundry detergents break up bloodstains and food stains. Others break down fats into smaller molecules, which can then be washed away. Soaps do the same thing but at a much higher temperature. Enzymes make cold-water washes possible, so they save energy. They are also biodegradable. Dirty wash water containing this kind of detergent is not harmful to the environment.

These detergent granules also demonstrate a new technology called *microencapsulation,* in which tiny particles of one material are surrounded by a shell of another. In the case of detergents the enzyme core is encapsulated by a shell of a water-soluble material. The enzymes are released only when you're doing the wash. Other examples of microencapsulation include scratch-and-sniff perfume ads in magazines and carbonless copy paper where the pressure of a pen produces a copy on the underlying sheet of paper.

TOOTHPASTE ABRASIVES

Remember the plaque we showed you earlier? Well, the best way to get rid of it is to brush daily. But brushing alone won't do it. You need an abrasive in your toothpaste. The abrasives in this SEM include mineral crystals of *dicalcium phosphate*—a delicate abrasive that won't harm tooth enamel. Several other abrasive minerals have been used on teeth. At one time, ground-up pumice was included in toothpaste. Today pumice is used by dentists only under special circumstances when they are trying to clean a particularly tough stain.

The abrasives in this micrograph are mixed with a gel, foaming agents, sweeteners, and flavoring in the manufacture of commercial toothpaste.

Making the Pictures

An ordinary light microscope can show us only structures that are thin enough to let light pass through them. At best, it can only enlarge an object about fourteen hundred times its actual size. The most highly magnified picture in this book is the gold crystal on page 5. It was taken with a kind of electron microscope that sends beams of electrons through a very, very thin slice of material. The image is later made sharper by a computer.

The scanning electron microscope, used to take most of the pictures in this book, shows the surfaces of structures in three dimensions rather than a slice through them. The most highly magnified SEM is of the spider spinnerets on page 14.

The scanning electron microscope doesn't look anything like an ordinary microscope. For one thing, it's a lot larger. For another, it has a lot more parts to it. This is a picture of Dennis Kunkel, a University of Hawaii microscopist, sitting at his electron microscope, which he has affectionately named "Zoom." The picture he sees of the specimen is on the TV viewing screen on the panel in front of him. The television picture is created by a tiny beam of electrons—negatively charged particles— that scans back and forth in lines across a TV screen. The scanning is so fast, sixty times a second, that you see it as if the entire screen is lit up all at once. A similar type of scanning is used in the electron microscope.

The top of the long cylinder on Dennis's left contains an electron gun, which shoots a stream of electrons at a specimen below it. The specimen is coated with a thin layer of gold before it is placed in the specimen chamber below the gun. The entire insides of the microscope are connected to a vacuum pump because air interferes with the path of the electrons. When the electron beam is scanned over the specimen, it excites the gold molecules to release their electrons. These excited electrons are collected and sent to the TV viewing screen. The pattern of the electrons shows up as light and shadow on the screen. The black-

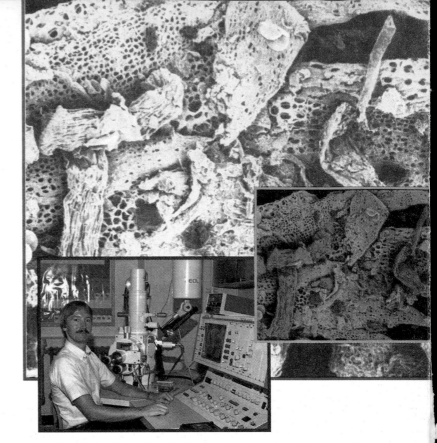

and-white picture looks like a bird's-eye view of the specimen's surface.

When he finds an image he likes on the screen, Dennis can take a photograph called a micrograph. The scanning electron microscope can produce only a black-and-white image like the large micrograph of humus. It is colored later by hand or by computer. The artists who do the coloring must know what they're looking at in order to color the black-and-white image.